T0160933

My First Japanese Kanji Book

Learning kanji the fun and easy way!

はじめての漢字の本

Written by Anna Sato and Eriko Sato
Illustrated by Anna Sato

TUTTLE PUBLISHING
Tokyo • Rutland, Vermont • Singapore

To Anna's late grandfather, Yoshio Sato

Acknowledgments

The authors are grateful to Anna's grandfather, the late Yoshio Sato, and her grandmother, Etsuko Sato, in Japan, as well as the students of the Pre-College Japanese Program at the State University of New York at Stony Brook, for inspiring them to write this book for English/Japanese bilingual children and for others interested in learning basic kanji in context. Being able to talk with one's grandparents and relatives to express love and share culture and tradition is a special life-time treasure to be cherished by one's entire family, and ultimately becomes a life-time strength.

The creation of this book involved an enjoyable mother-daughter collaboration through language teaching and learning. Special thanks to Anna's cousin, Kota Motonaga, and his parents, Yoshinori and Yumiko Motonaga, for their continued and selfless help. The authors are also grateful to Anna's art teacher, June Adinolfi, for enthusiastically and effectively guiding her to create all 36 illustrations in this book over the past four years, and to Tuttle's editors, Bob Graham and Sandra Korinchak, and the designer, Sook Fan Loh, for their professionalism, dedication, and kindness. Last but not least, special heartfelt thanks to Yimei Zhu, Anna's father and Eriko's husband, for his never-ending support and for being excited about this book with us.

Published by Tuttle Publishing, an imprint of Periplus Editions (HK) Ltd., with editorial offices at 364 Innovation Drive, North Clarendon, Vermont 05759 U.S.A.

Copyright © 2009 by Periplus Editions (HK) Ltd.

All rights reserved. No part of this publication may be reproduced or utilized in any form or by any means, electronic or mechanical, including photocopying, recording, or by any information storage and retrieval system, without prior written permission from the publisher.

Library of Congress Cataloging-in-Publication Data

Sato, Anna.
My first Japanese Kanji book : learn Kanji the fun and easy way! / written by Anna Sato and Eriko Sato ; illustrated by Anna Sato.
p. cm.
ISBN 978-4-8053-1037-3 (alk. paper)
1. Chinese characters--Japan. 2. Japanese language--Orthography and spelling. I. Sato, Eriko, 1962- II. Title.
PL528.S37 2009
495.6'82421--dc22
2008055783

First edition
13 12 11 10 09 10 9 8 7 6 5 4 3 2 1

Distributed by:

North America, Latin America & Europe
Tuttle Publishing
364 Innovation Drive, North Clarendon,
VT 05759-9436 U.S.A
Tel: 1 (802) 773 8930Fax: 1 (802) 773 6993
info@tuttlepublishing.com
www.tuttlepublishing.com

Japan
Tuttle Publishing
Yaekari Building, 3rd Floor, 5-4-12 Osaki,
Shinagawa-ku, Tokyo 141 0032
Tel: (81) 3 5437-0171; Fax: (81) 3 5437-0755
tuttle-sales@gol.com

Asia-Pacific
Berkeley Books Pte Ltd
61 Tai Seng Avenue #02-12, Singapore 534167
Tel: (65) 6280-3320; Fax: (65) 6280-6290
inquiries@periplus.com.sg
www.periplus.com

ISBN: 978-4-8053-1037-3

Printed in Singapore

TUTTLE PUBLISHING® is a registered trademark of Tuttle Publishing, a division of Periplus Editions (HK) Ltd.

CONTENTS

Preface 5

Lesson 1 からて Karate (一・二・三) 6

Lesson 2 こうえん Park (Playground) (人・子) 7

Lesson 3 おじいちゃんのいなか My Grandpa's Inaka (山・川) 8

Lesson 4 お日さまと、お月さま The Sun and the Moon (日・月・明) 10

Lesson 5 いもうと My Little Sister (目・口・見) 12

Lesson 6 木のあるところ Places with Trees (木・林・森) 14

Lesson 7 はな火 Sparklers (火・光・水) 16

Lesson 8 車りん Wheels (車・自) 17

Lesson 9 田んぼ Rice Fields (田・土・米) 18

Lesson 10 金メダル Gold Medal (金・銀) 20

Lesson 11 大きい犬と、小さい犬 A Big Dog and a Small Dog（大・小・犬）.....21
Lesson 12 かがみ Mirror（右・左・中）.....22
Lesson 13 シーソー Seesaw（上・下・兄）.....24
Lesson 14 男の子と、女の子 Boys and Girls（男・女・好）.....26
Lesson 15 字をつかって Using Letters（字・文・本・書）.....28
Lesson 16 学校 School（学・校）.....30
Lesson 17 私の先生 My Teacher（私・先・生）.....31
Lesson 18 正正堂堂 Acting Right, Playing Fair（四・年・正）.....32
Lesson 19 サッカーボール Soccer Ball（五・六・角・形）.....34
Lesson 20 インデアン・ボーイズ Indian Boys（七・八・九・十）.....36
Lesson 21 おこづかい My Allowance（百・千・円・玉）.....38
Lesson 22 どうぶつ Animals（手・足・耳・長）.....40
Lesson 23 力を使って Using My Strength（体・力・使）.....42
Lesson 24 出る人と、入る人 People Who Exit and People Who Enter（入・出・電）.....43
Lesson 25 休むとき When Resting（立・休・強）.....44
Lesson 26 はた Flags（白・赤・青）.....45
Lesson 27 貝の名前 The Names of Shellfish（貝・名・前・何）.....46
Lesson 28 早おき Getting Up Early（早・朝）.....48
Lesson 29 夕がたの空 The Sky at Dusk（夕・空・帰）.....49
Lesson 30 春ののはら Spring Field（草・花・春）.....50
Lesson 31 竹 Bamboo（竹・馬・歩）.....52
Lesson 32 虫の音楽会 Bugs' Concert（虫・音・夜）.....54
Lesson 33 村と、町 Villages and Towns（村・町・家・店）.....56
Lesson 34 宝石 Gemstones（王・石・宝）.....58
Lesson 35 糸 Threads（糸・毛・作）.....60
Lesson 36 てるてるぼうず Teru-Teru Bozu（雨・天・気）.....62
Hiragana and Katakana charts 64

PREFACE

This kanji book introduces 109 kanji characters to Japanese or Japanese-English bilingual children (kindergarten or elementary school) who have already mastered hiragana and katakana, and who want to learn kanji for the first time with culturally rich and age-appropriate poems and illustrations. It includes all the first grade level kanji characters and some second to sixth grade kanji characters. This book can be used as a self-study text, a teaching material by parents or tutors, a supplementary material in overseas Japanese language schools, or a gift book from family, relatives, or friends.

The kanji characters are introduced according to their degree of relevance to children's daily lives as well as according to the degree of complexity of the characters. The information provided for each character (pronunciation, stroke order, usage examples, and English translations) is kept to a minimum so that it will not overwhelm young learners of kanji. There are 36 lessons; each lesson introduces two to four kanji characters and a poem that uses them. The poems reflect children's viewpoints or Japanese parents' childhood memories, and are short and easy to read aloud, memorize, and recite. As they read the poems, children can experience Japanese culture, recognize concepts and values in Japanese society, develop curiosity about nature (animals, landscapes, weather, universe, body, health, life, etc.), and think of their social relationships with family, friends, schoolmates, and teachers. Each poem is accompanied by a friendly illustration to help children understand, enjoy, visualize, and remember it.

Children can study a lesson each day or each week. Furigana (pronunciation guides for kanji characters) and English translations are provided for each of the poems. By reading the poems repeatedly without relying on furigana and translations, children reinforce their acquisition of kanji. In addition, each new kanji is accompanied by stroke-order diagrams, sample vocabulary, and boxes for writing practice. Children may also use the accompanying MP3 audio CD to listen to the poems read in Japanese and in English. It is our hope that children will attain a feeling of accomplishment by completing all the lessons and learning to read the poems with new kanji confidently.

からて Karate (一・二・三)

からての　れんしゅう
Practicing karate;

いち　に　さん
一、二、三。
one, two, three.

からだを　きたえる
Strengthening my body;

いち　に　さん
一、二、三。
one, two, three.

こころも　きたえる
Strengthening my spirit, too;

いち　に　さん
一、二、三。
one, two, three.

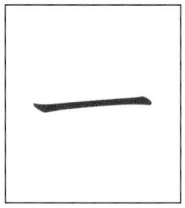

one

[kun] ひと-つ
[on] イチ

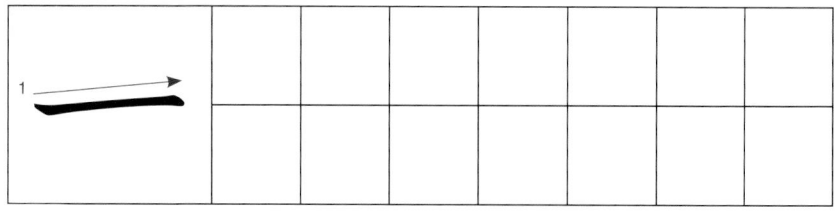

いち	ひと	いちじ	いちばん	いちがつついたち
一	一つ	一時	一番	一月一日
one	one (thing)	one o'clock	number one, the best	January 1st

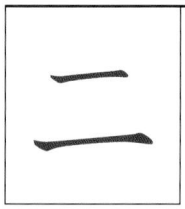

two

[kun] ふた-つ
[on] ニ

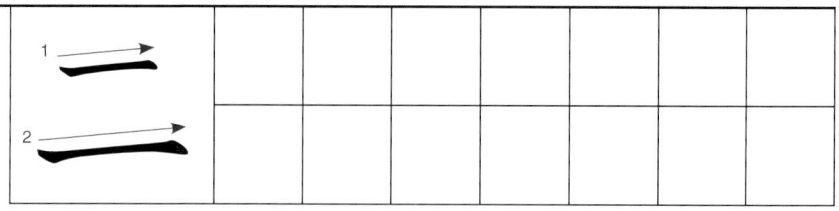

に	ふた	にじ	にがつふつか
二	二つ	二時	二月二日
two	two (things)	two o'clock	February 2nd

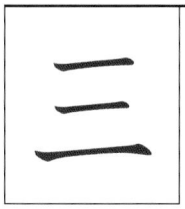

three

[kun] みっ-つ
[on] サン

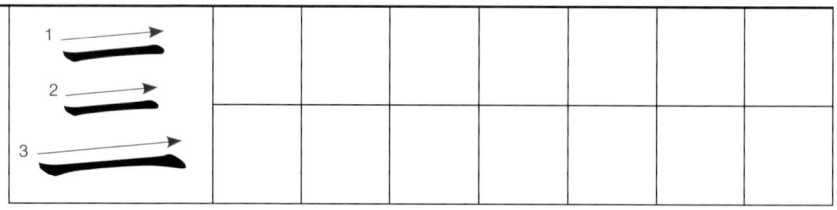

さん	みっ	さんじ	さんがつみっか	みかづき
三	三つ	三時	三月三日	三日月
three	three (things)	three o'clock	March 3rd	crescent moon

こうえん Park (Playground) (人・子)

きょうは　おてんき。
It's a nice day.

ここは　こうえん。
This is a playground.

あっ、おとこの子(こ)が　いる。
Oh, there are boys.

一人(ひとり)、二人(ふたり)、三人(さんにん)。
One, two, three.

だれか　ぼくと　あそんでくれないかな。
I wonder if somebody would play with me.

ゆうきを　だして、「あそぼう」って、
いって みようかな。
I wonder if I should gather my courage and ask them,
"Can I play with you?"

人	man, person **[kun]** ひと **[on]** ジン／ニン

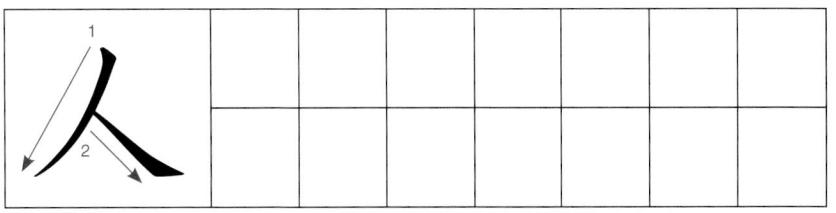

あの人(ひと)
that person

男(おとこ)の人(ひと)
man

女(おんな)の人(ひと)
woman

アメリカ人(じん)
American person

日本人(にほんじん)
Japanese person

外国人(がいこくじん)
foreigner

人間(にんげん)
human being

主人(しゅじん)
one's own husband

一人(ひとり)、二人(ふたり)、三人(さんにん)、四人(よにん)、五人(ごにん)
one, two, three, four, five person(s)

子	child **[kun]** こ **[on]** シ

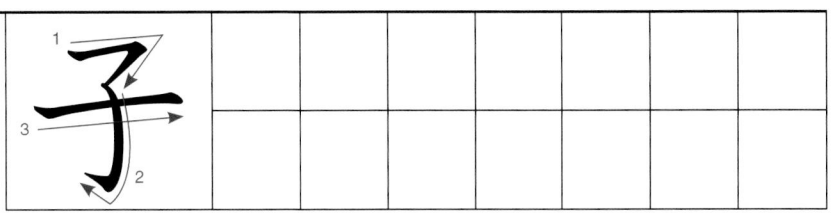

子(こ)ども
child

男(おとこ)の子(こ)
boy

女(おんな)の子(こ)
girl

女子学生(じょしがくせい)
female student

おじいちゃんの いなか My Grandpa's Inaka (山・川)

おじいちゃんの　いなかは　くうきが　おいしい。
The air tastes good in my grandpa's inaka (hometown in the countryside).

山(やま)が　ある。
There are mountains.

川(かわ)も　ある。
There are also rivers.

山(やま)に　いって、さんさいを　とる。
We go to the mountain, and pick wild vegetables.

川(かわ)に　いって、さかなを　つる。
We go to the river, and fish.

また、なつに　なったら、いきたいな。おじいちゃんの　いなか。
When the summer comes again, I want to go back to my grandpa's inaka.

山	mountain **[kun]** やま **[on]** サン	山						

ふじさん	さんちょう	やまのぼり	やまぐに	やまだ
富士山	山頂	山登り	山国	山田さん
Mt. Fuji	summit	mountain climbing	mountainous country	Mr./Ms./Mrs. Yamada

川	river **[kun]** かわ／-がわ **[on]** (セン)	川						

かわ	おがわ	とねがわ	ナイルがわ	かわぐち
川	小川	利根川	ナイル川	川口さん
river	brook, stream	the Tone River	the Nile River	Mr./Ms./Mrs. Kawaguchi

お日(ひ)さまと、お月(つき)さま The Sun and the Moon (日・月・明)

お日(ひ)さまは　ぼくが　そとで　あそんでるとき、
いつも　いっしょに　いてくれる。
When I'm playing outside, the sun is always with me.

お月(つき)さまは　おとうさんが　おうちに　かえるとき、
いつも　いっしょに　ついてきてくれる。
When my dad comes home, the moon always comes with him.

お日(ひ)さまと、お月(つき)さまは　いつも　たかい　ところから、
ぼくたちを　みていてくれる。
The sun and the moon always watch over us from high up there.

いつも　たかい　ところから、ぼくたちの　まわりを　明(あか)るく　してくれる。
They always brighten the place around us from high up there.

すごいな。
They are amazing!

かみさまみたい。
They are like gods!

日	sun, day **[kun]** ひ／び／か **[on]** ニチ／ニ／ジツ	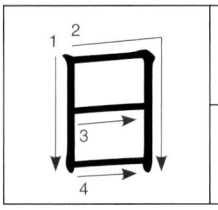

ひ
日
sun, day

に ほん(にっぽん)
日本
Japan

にちようび
日曜日
Sunday

きょう
今日
today

月	moon, month **[kun]** つき **[on]** ゲツ・ガツ	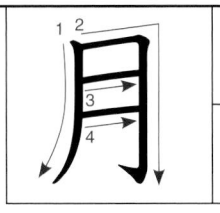

つき
月
moon, month

まんげつ
満月
full moon

げつようび
月曜日
Monday

らいげつ
来月
next month

いちがつ
一月
January

いっ げつ
一か月
one month

明	bright **[kun]** あかーるい／あーける／あきーらか **[on]** メイ	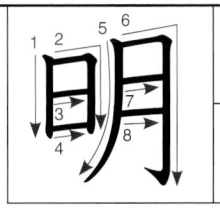

あか
明るい
bright, cheerful

あし た
明日
tomorrow

はつめい
発明
invention

ぶんめい
文明
civilization

いもうと My Little Sister (目・口・見)

いもうとは　うれしくなると、目(め)が　たれちゃう。
When my little sister becomes happy, her eyes turn into lines slightly slanted down.

いもうとは　おこると、口(くち)が　とんがっちゃう。
When my little sister gets mad, her mouth is pursed.

いもうとは　ねると、口(くち)も、目(め)も、つむっちゃう。
When my little sister sleeps, both her eyes and mouth close.

いいゆめ　見(み)てね。ななちゃん。
Sweet dreams, Nana-chan.

目	eye, item **[kun]** め **[on]** モク	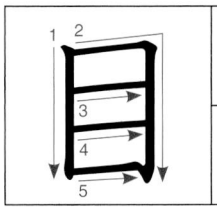

め
目
eye

め ざ ど けい
目覚まし時計
alarm clock

もくひょう
目標
aim, goal

もくじ
目次
table of contents

口	mouth **[kun]** くち／ぐち **[on]** コウ	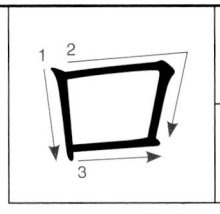

くち
口
mouth

くちべに
口紅
lipstick

くちぶえ
口笛をふく
to whistle

じんこう
人口
population

見	look, see, view **[kun]** み-る／み-える／み-せる **[on]** ケン	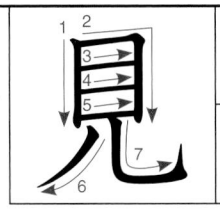

み
見る
to look at

み
見せる
to show

はっけん
発見
discovery

いけん
意見
opinion

木(き)のあるところ Places with Trees (木・林・森)

林(はやし)の　なかは　しずかで、すずしくて、きもちいい。
In the woods, it is quiet, cool, and soothing.

かぜが　木(き)と木(き)の　あいだを　すうっと　とおる。
The breeze can pass through the trees.

ぼくも　かけまわる。
I can run through the trees, too.

森(もり)の　なかは　いろんな木(き)が　ごちゃごちゃ　している。
The forest is crowded with all sorts of trees.

森(もり)の　なかは　えだを　かきわけながら　あるく。
As I walk, I need to slash my way through the forest.

まいごに　なったら、くまさんに　あうかも。
If I get lost, I may encounter Mr. Bear!

木	tree **[kun]** き **[on]** モク／ボク	木						

き
木
tree, wood

もくようび
木曜日
Thursday

もくせい
木星
Jupiter

ぼくとう
木刀
wooden sword

林	wood, grove **[kun]** はやし **[on]** リン	林						

はやし
林
woods

まつばやし
松林
pinewood

はやし
林さん
Mr./Ms./Mrs. Hayashi

森	forest, jungle **[kun]** もり **[on]** シン	森						

もり
森
forest

しんりん
森林
woods and forests

もり
森さん
Mr./Ms./Mrs. Mori

はな火(び) Sparklers (火・光・水)

なつの　よるは　はな火(び)を　します。
On a summer night, we play with sparklers.

ちいさい　光(ひかり)が　キラキラ、パチパチ。
Tiny lights sparkle and crackle.

ゆめみたいに　きれい。
Like a dream, it's beautiful.

はな火(び)を　するときは　おとなの人(ひと)と
しましょう。
When you play with sparklers,
you must do so with adults.

バケツの　水(みず)も　わすれないようにね。
Don't forget a bucket of water, too.

火	fire **[kun]** ひ **[on]** カ	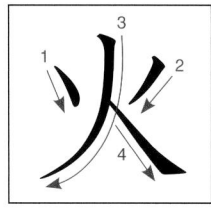						

火(ひ)	火曜日(かようび)	火星(かせい)	花火(はなび)	火山(かざん)	火事(かじ)
fire, flame	Tuesday	Mars	fireworks	volcano	fire (destructive burning)

光	light, shine **[kun]** ひかり／ひかーる **[on]** コウ	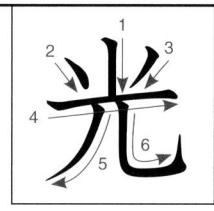						

光(ひかり)	光る(ひかる)	日光(にっこう)
light	to shine	sunlight

水	water **[kun]** みず **[on]** スイ	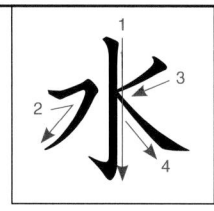						

水(みず)	噴水(ふんすい)	水曜日(すいようび)	水星(すいせい)	水泳(すいえい)
water	fountain	Wednesday	Mercury	swimming

車(しゃ)りん Wheels (車・自)

うば車(ぐるま)に、ておし車(ぐるま)。
A baby carriage and a wheelbarrow.

さんりん車(しゃ)に、自(じ)てん車(しゃ)に、いちりん車(しゃ)。
A tricycle, a bicycle, and a unicycle.

それから、でん車(しゃ)に、自(じ)どう車(しゃ)。
A train and a car!

ぜんぶ　車(しゃ)りんが　ついてます。
All of them have wheels.

ぜんぶ　車(くるま)と　いう　じが　ついてます。
All of them have the character *kuruma* (車).

車

car

[kun] くるま
[on] シャ

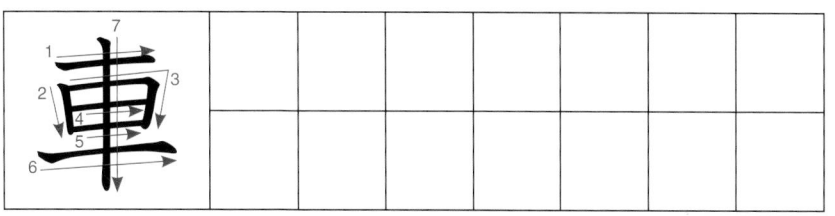

車(くるま)	自動車(じどうしゃ)	自転車(じてんしゃ)	車輪(しゃりん)	歯車(はぐるま)
car	automobile	bicycle	wheel	gear

自

self

[kun] みずから
[on] ジ／シ

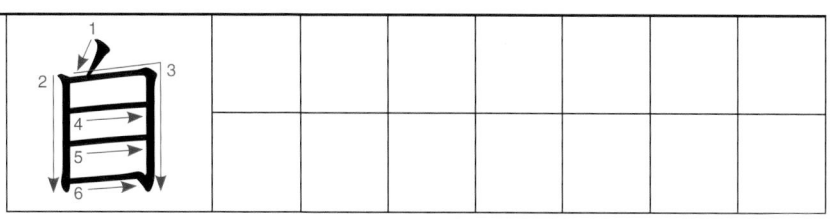

自分(じぶん)	自由(じゆう)	自信(じしん)	自然(しぜん)	自宅(じたく)
self	freedom	confidence	nature	one's own house/home

田(た)んぼ Rice Fields (田・土・米)

三(さん)じかん　でん車(しゃ)に　のって、きたに　いくと、
いつのまにか　田(た)んぼが　つづく。
If I take a train and go north for three hours, all I see are rice fields.

田(た)んぼの　田(た)の　じは　田(た)んぼの　かたち。
The character 田 in 田んぼ (rice field) has the shape of a rice field.

田(た)んぼで　お米(こめ)を　つくります。
We make rice in a rice field.

はるの　田(た)んぼは　土(つち)の　いろ。
Rice fields in the spring are the color of the soil.

なつの　田(た)んぼは　みどりいろ。
Rice fields in the summer are green in color.

あきの　田(た)んぼは　こがねいろ。
Rice fields in the fall are gold in color.

ふゆの　田(た)んぼは　ゆきの　いろ。
Rice fields in the winter are the color of the snow.

田	rice field **[kun]** た／だ **[on]** デン	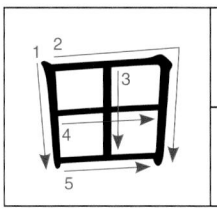

田んぼ	田舎	油田	山田さん
rice paddies	countryside	oil field	Mr./Ms./Mrs. Yamada

土	soil, ground, earth **[kun]** つち **[on]** ド／ト	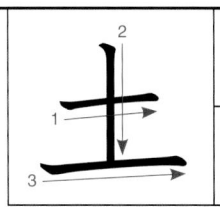

土	粘土	土曜日	土星	土地
soil	clay	Saturday	Saturn	(piece of) land

米	rice **[kun]** こめ **[on]** マイ／ベイ	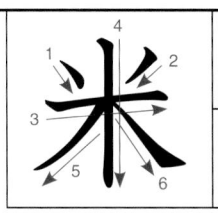

米	玄米	白米	米国
rice	brown (unpolished) rice	white (polished) rice	U.S.A.

金(きん)メダル Gold Medal (金・銀)

一(いち)ばん　よく　できた人(ひと)は
The person who did the best

金(きん)メダルを　もらいます。
receives the gold medal.

二(に)ばん目(め)に　よく　できた人(ひと)は
The person who did the second best

銀(ぎん)メダルを　もらいます。
receives the silver medal.

三(さん)ばん目(め)に　よく　できた人(ひと)は
The person who did the third best

銅(どう)メダルを　もらいます。
receives the bronze medal.

いっしょうけんめい　やれば、
メダルを　もらえなくても、えらいです。
Even if you could not receive a medal,
you did a great job if you tried your best.

金	gold, money, metal **[kun]** かね **[on]** キン	金 (1–8)						

金(きん) gold　金メダル(きんメダル) gold medal　お金(かね) money　金属(きんぞく) metal　金曜日(きんようび) Friday　金星(きんせい) Venus

銀	silver **[kun]** none **[on]** ギン	銀 (1–14)						

銀(ぎん) silver　銀メダル(ぎんメダル) silver medal　銀色(ぎんいろ) silver color　銀行(ぎんこう) bank　銀河系(ぎんがけい) the Milky Way galaxy

大(おお)きい犬(いぬ)と、小(ちい)さい犬(いぬ)

A Big Dog and a Small Dog (大・小・犬)

大(おお)きい　犬(いぬ)は　ゆっくり　あるきます。
A big dog walks slowly (with big steps).

小(ちい)さい　犬(いぬ)は　はやあしで　あるきます。
A small dog walks quickly (with many tiny steps).

大(おお)きい　犬(いぬ)は　ゆっくり　ワンと　ほえます。
A big dog barks slowly, "Wan".

小(ちい)さい　犬(いぬ)は　はやくちで
キャン　キャンと　ほえます。
A small dog barks quickly, "Kyan Kyan".

大	big, large, great **[kun]** おお-きい **[on]** ダイ／タイ

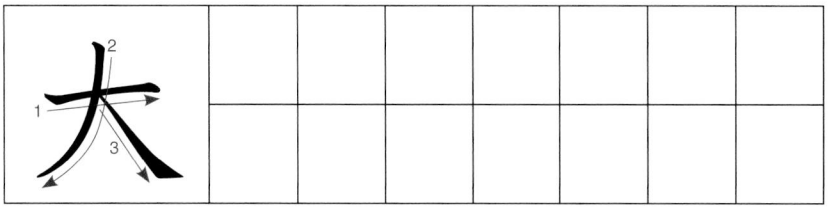

大(おお)きい big　　大学(だいがく) university　　大人(おとな) adult　　大切(たいせつ)な important

小	small, little **[kun]** ちい-さい／こ／お **[on]** ショウ

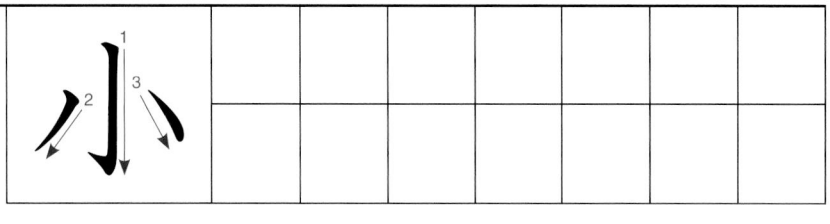

小(ちい)さい small　　小学生(しょうがくせい) elementary school student　　小川(おがわ) a brook, a stream　　小説(しょうせつ) novel

犬	dog **[kun]** いぬ **[on]** ケン

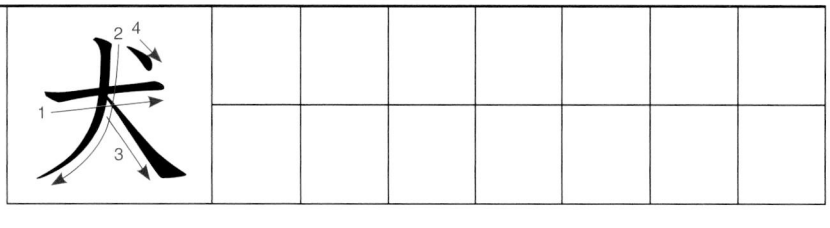

犬(いぬ) dog　　子犬(こいぬ) puppy　　番犬(ばんけん) watch dog　　野良犬(のらいぬ) stray dog

かがみ Mirror (右・左・中)

右(みぎ)てを　あげた。
I raised my right hand,

でも、かがみの　中(なか)では　左(ひだり)てが　あがった。
but my left hand rose in the mirror.

左目(ひだりめ)で　ウインクした。
I winked with my left eye,

でも、かがみの　中(なか)では　右目(みぎめ)で　ウインク。
but my right eye winked in the mirror.

さかだちした。
I did a hand stand.

こんどは　かがみの　中(なか)でも　さかだち。
This time, I was also doing a hand stand in the mirror.

どうして、はんたいに　なるのは　右(みぎ)と、左(ひだり)だけなんだろう？
I wonder, why do only right and left switch?

右

right

[kun] みぎ
[on] ユウ／ウ

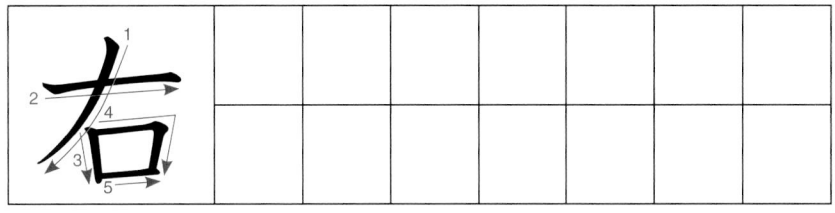

みぎ
右
right

みぎき
右利き
right-handed person

うせつ
右折する
to turn right

左

left

[kun] ひだり
[on] サ

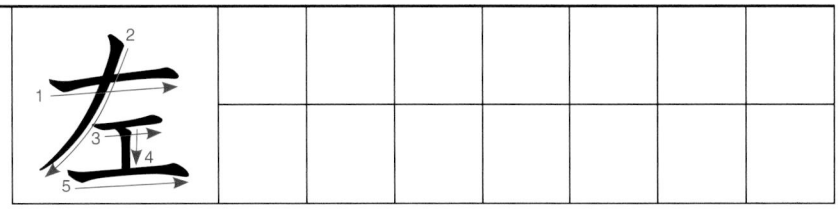

ひだり
左
left

させつ
左折する
to turn left

さゆう
左右
right and left

中

middle, inside

[kun] なか
[on] チュウ

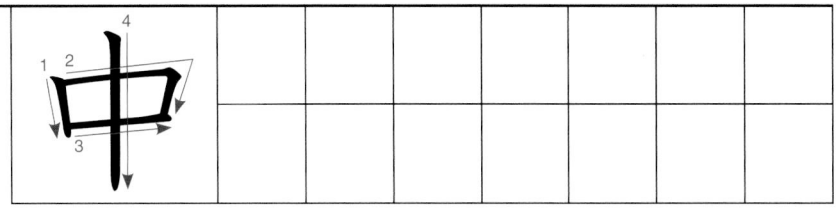

かばんの中（なか）
inside the bag

ちゅうがくせい
中学生
junior high school student

ちゅうしん
中心
center

ちゅうかんしけん
中間試験
mid-term exam

シーソー Seesaw (上・下・兄)

ギッタン　バッコン　ギッタン　バッコン
Gittan bakkon gittan bakkon

お兄(にい)ちゃんが　下(さ)がると、わたしが　上(あ)がる。
When my brother goes down, I go up.

わたしが　下(さ)がると、お兄(にい)ちゃんが　上(あ)がる。
When I go down, my brother goes up.

上(うえ)に いって、下(した)に いって 。
Going up, going down.

下(した)に いって、上(うえ)に いって。
Going down, going up.

ギッタン　バッコン　ギッタン　バッコン
Gittan bakkon gittan bakkon

上	above, on, up, superior **[kun]** うえ／あ-がる／のぼ-る／あ-げる **[on]** ジョウ

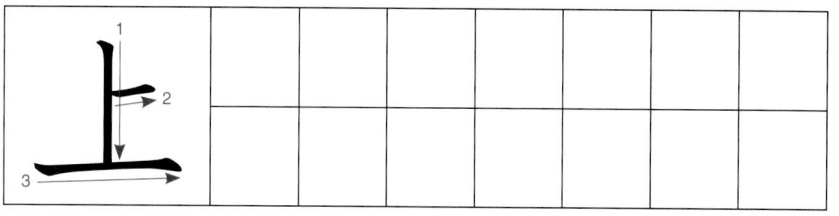

テーブルの上（うえ）
on the table

上がる（あ）
to go up

上手（じょうず）
skillful

上り電車（のぼ でんしゃ）
in-bound train

屋上（おくじょう）
housetop, roof

下	under, down, inferior **[kun]** した／さ-がる／くだ-る／さ-げる **[on]** カ／ゲ

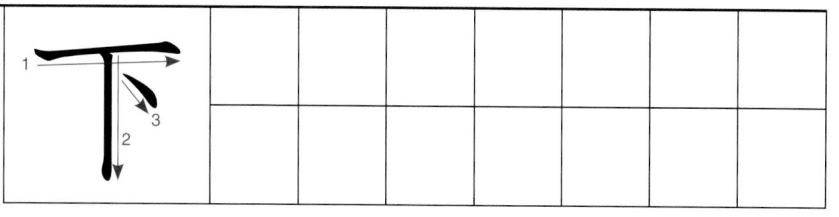

テーブルの下（した）
under the table

下がる（さ）
to go down

下手（へた）
unskillful

下り電車（くだ でんしゃ）
out-bound train

地下（ちか）
underground

下駄（げた）
Japanese wooden clogs

兄	elder brother **[kun]** あに／お-にい-さん **[on]** ケイ／キョウ

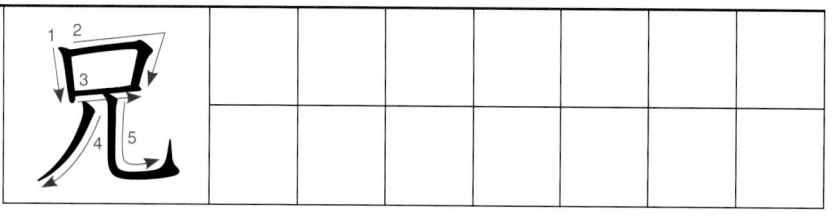

兄（あに）
one's elder brother

お兄さん（にい）
elder brother

兄弟（きょうだい）
siblings

男の子と、女の子 Boys and Girls (男・女・好)

男の子は　たいてい　おにごっこが　好き。
Boys usually like to play tag.

女の子は　たいてい　ままごとが　好き。
Girls usually like to play house.

でも、女の子も　ときどき　おにごっこを　します。
But sometimes, girls also play tag.

男の子も　ときどき　ままごとを　します。
Sometimes, boys also play house.

男	man, male **[kun]** おとこ **[on]** ダン／ナン	男						

おとこ ひと
男の人
man

おとこ こ
男の子
boy

ちょうなん
長男
eldest son

女	woman, female **[kun]** おんな **[on]** ジョ	女						

おんな ひと
女の人
woman

おんな こ
女の子
girl

かのじょ
彼女
she

じょゆう
女優
actress

好	love, like, favorite **[kun]** す-きな／す-く **[on]** コウ	好						

す
好きな
favorite

す きら
好き嫌い
likes and dislikes

こうきしん
好奇心
curiosity

字(じ)をつかって Using Letters (字・文・本・書)

あいうえおは　日本(にほん)の字(じ)。
あ, い, う, え, and お are Japanese letters.

アメリカの字(じ)は　ABC。
American letters are A, B, and C.

字(じ)が　あるから、文(ぶん)が　書(か)ける。
Because we have letters, we can write a sentence.

文(ぶん)を　つなげると、おはなしに　なる。
If we connect sentences, we can make a story.

おもしろいと、本(ほん)にも　なる。
If it is interesting, it becomes a book.

わすれないうちに、おもったことを　書(か)いておこう。
Before we forget, let's write down our thoughts.

字	letter, character **[kun]** none **[on]** ジ	字						

じ
字
letter, character

かんじ
漢字
kanji (Chinese characters)

すうじ
数字
numbers

しゅうじ
習字
penmanship

文	sentence, literature **[kun]** ふみ **[on]** ブン／モン	文						

ぶん
文
sentence

ぶんか
文化
culture

もじ
文字
character, letter

ぶんがく
文学
literature

本	origin, main, book **[kun]** もと **[on]** ホン	本						

ほん
本
book

えほん
絵本
picture book

ほんとう
本当の
true, real

書	write, book, document **[kun]** かーく **[on]** ショ	書						

か
書く
to write

しょどう
書道
calligraphy

きょうかしょ
教科書
textbook

学校 School (学・校)

がっこう　かわ　なか
めだかの学校は　川の中。
The fishes' school is in the river.

がっこう　つち　なか
ありの学校は　土の中。
The ants' school is in the ground.

がっこう　なか
たこの学校は　うみの中。
The octopi's school is in the ocean.

がっこう　もり　なか
くまの学校は　森の中。
The bears' school is in the forest.

がっこう　なか
ぼくの学校は　まちの中。
My school is in the town.

学

study

[kun] まな-ぶ
[on] ガク／ガッ

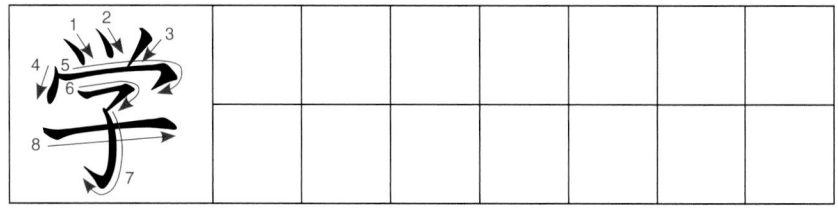

まな
学ぶ
to learn

がくせい
学生
student

がくしゃ
学者
scholar

がくしゅう
学習
learning

すうがく
数学
mathematics

にゅうがく
入学
admission into a school

校

school

[kun] none
[on] コウ

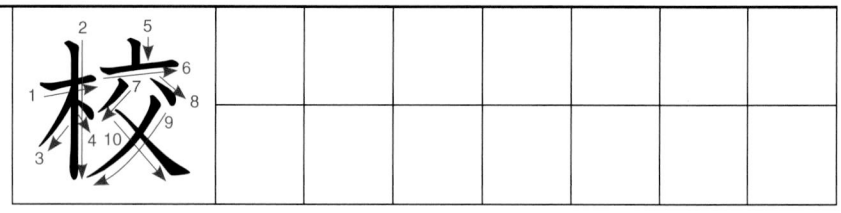

がっこう
学校
school

こうちょう
校長
school principal

こうこうせい
高校生
high school student

こうしゃ
校舎
school building

こうてい
校庭
school grounds

こうもん
校門
school gate

こうせい
校正
proofreading

私の先生 My Teacher (私・先・生)

私の先生は
My teacher

いつも　私の　はなしを
よく　きいてくれます。
always listens to what I say.

それから、いつも　私に
「がんばって」って、いってくれます。
She also always tells me, "Try your best!"

先生、ありがとう。
Thank you, Teacher!

私	private **[kun]** わたし／わたくし **[on]** シ

私

わたし
私
I

しどう
私道
private road (path)

しりつだいがく
私立大学
private university

先	ahead, previous **[kun]** さき **[on]** セン

さき
先に
on ahead

せんせい
先生
teacher

せんげつ
先月
last month

せんしゅう
先週
last week

せんぱい
先輩
one's senior

生	live, birth **[kun]** い-きる／う-まれる **[on]** セイ／ショウ

い
生きる
to live

う
生まれる
to be born

いっしょう
一生
lifetime

たんじょうび
誕生日
birthday

せいねんがっぴ
生年月日
date of birth

正正堂堂(せいせいどうどう) Acting Right, Playing Fair (四・年・正)

こうたくんは、小学校(しょうがっこう)の　四年生(よねんせい)。
Kōta is a 4th grader in elementary school.

正(ただ)しいと　おもったことは、正正堂堂(せいせいどうどう)と　やります。
Whenever there's something that he thinks is right, he does it boldly.

だれかが　まちがったことを　していたら、
Whenever there is someone who is doing something wrong,

正正堂堂(せいせいどうどう)と　ちゅういします。
he lets them know without hesitation.

じぶんが　まちがっていたら、正正堂堂(せいせいどうどう)と　あやまります。
Whenever he realizes that he is wrong, he apologizes valiantly.

やきゅうの　しあいでは、正正堂堂(せいせいどうどう)と　たたかいます。
Whenever he plays baseball, he competes fairly.

四

four

[kun]] よっ-つ／よん／よ
[on] シ

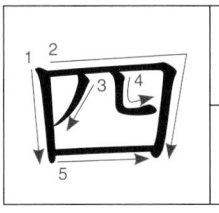

よっ
四つ
four (things)

よじ
四時
four o'clock

しがつよっか
四月四日
April 4th

しき
四季
four seasons

年

year, age

[kun] とし
[on] ネン

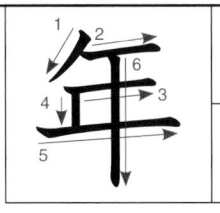

とし
年
year, age

としよ
お年寄り
elderly people

よねんせい
四年生
fourth grade

きょねん
去年
last year

らいねん
来年
next year

正

correct, right

[kun] ただ-しい
[on] セイ／ショウ

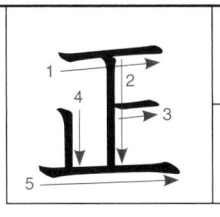

ただ
正しい
correct, right

せいかく
正確な
accurate

しょうがつ
正月
the New Year

せいぎ
正義
justice

しょうじき
正直な
honest

サッカーボール Soccer Ball (五・六・角・形)

ごかくけい　ろっかくけい
サッカーボールは、五角形と、六角形で、できている。
A soccer ball is made of pentagons and hexagons.

ごかくけい　ろっかくけい　いつ
五角形の　まわりには、六角形が　五つ　ある。
Each pentagon is surrounded by five hexagons.

ろっかくけい　ろっかくけい　み　ごかくけい　みっ
六角形の　まわりには、六角形が　三つと、五角形が　三つ　ある。
Each hexagon is surrounded by three hexagons and three pentagons.

ごかくけい　ろっかくけい
五角形と、六角形って、なかよしなんだな。
Pentagons and hexagons seem to get along very well.

ぴったり　くっついて、まんまるの　ボールを　つくってる。
They fit together perfectly to form a perfect ball!

五

five

[kun] いつ-つ
[on] ゴ

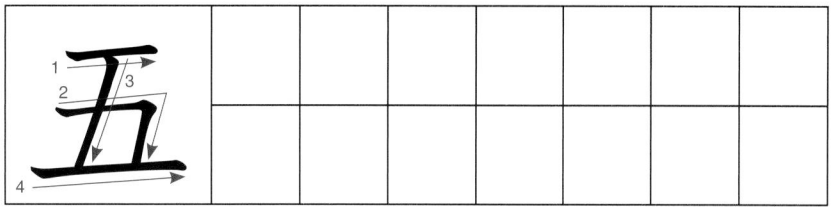

ご
五
five

いつ
五つ
five (things)

ごがついつか
五月五日
May 5th

ごかくけい
五角形
pentagon

六

six

[kun] むっ-つ
[on] ロク

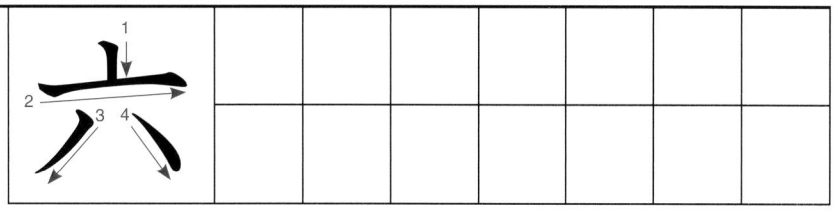

ろく
六
six

むっ
六つ
six (things)

ろくがつむいか
六月六日
June 6th

ろっかくけい
六角形
hexagon

角

angle, corner, horn

[kun] かど／つの
[on] カク

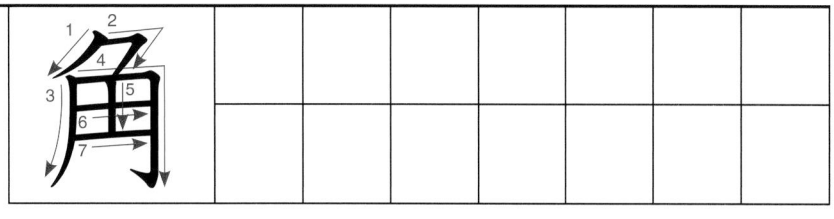

かど
角
corner

つの
角
horn

かくど
角度
angle

形

shape

[kun] かた／かたち
[on] ケイ／ギョウ

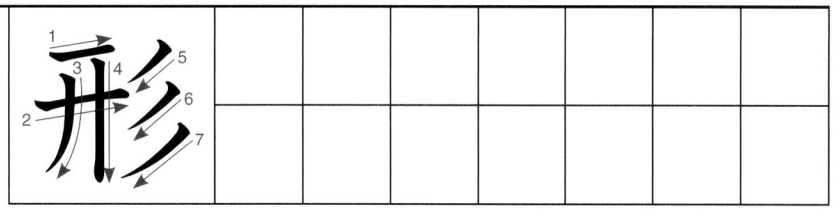

かたち
形
shape

さんかくけい
三角形
triangle

にんぎょう
人形
doll

インディアン・ボーイズ Indian Boys (七・八・九・十)

ひとり　ふたり　さんにん
一人、二人、三人の　インディアン
One little, two little, three little Indians

よんにん　ごにん　ろくにん
四人、五人、六人の　インディアン
Four little, five little, six little Indians

しちにん　はちにん　きゅうにん
七人、八人、九人の　インディアン
Seven little, eight little, nine little Indians

じゅうにん
十人の　インディアン・ボーイズ
Ten little Indian boys

七

seven

[kun] なな-つ
[on] シチ

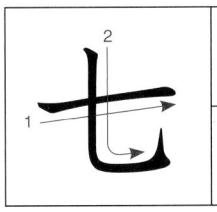

ななしち 七(七) seven	なな 七つ seven (things)	しちがつなのか 七月七日 July 7th

八

eight

[kun] やっ-つ
[on] ハチ

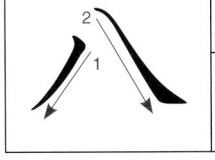

はち 八 eight	やっ 八つ eight (things)	はちがつようか 八月八日 August 8th

九

nine

[kun] ここの-つ
[on] ク／キュウ

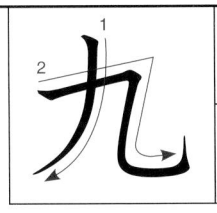

きゅう 九 nine	ここの 九つ nine (things)	くがつここのか 九月九日 September 9th

十

ten

[kun] とお
[on] ジュウ

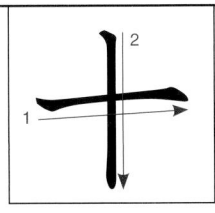

じゅう 十 ten	とお 十 ten (things)	じゅうがつとおか 十月十日 October 10th

おこづかい My Allowance (百・千・円・玉)

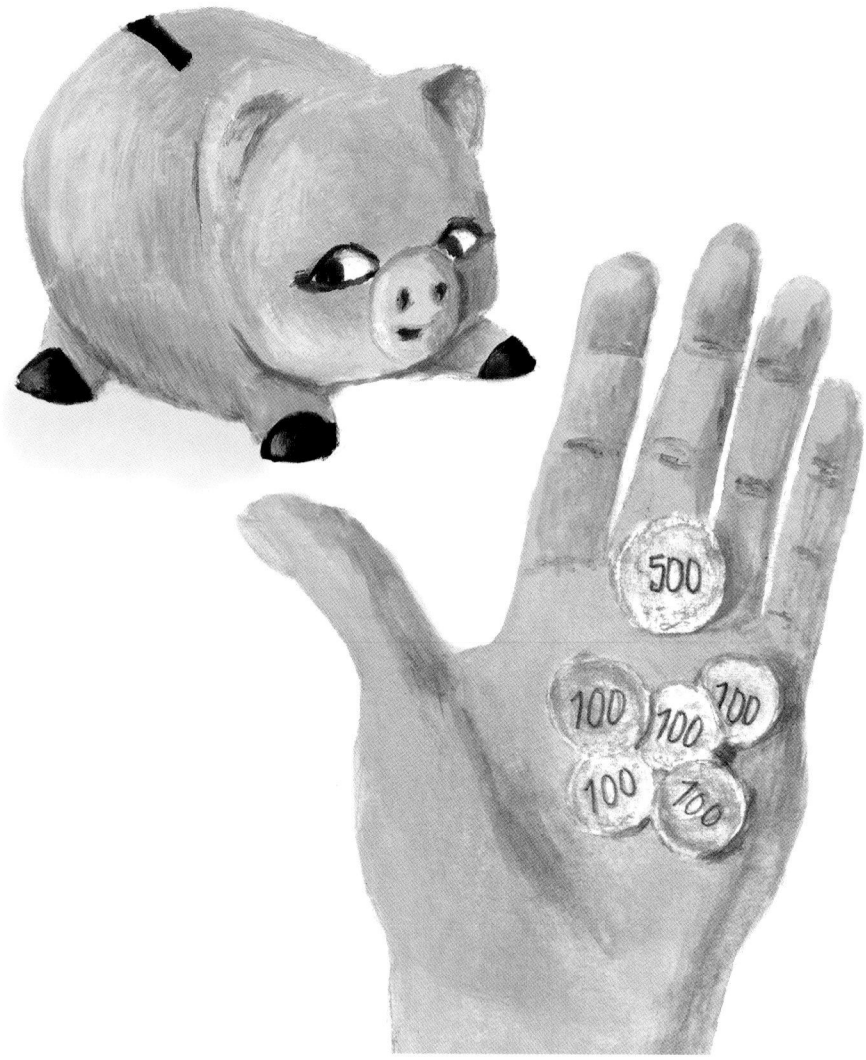

おとうさんが　百円玉(ひゃくえんだま)を　二(ふた)つ　くれました。
My dad gave me two one-hundred-yen coins.

おばあちゃんは　百円玉(ひゃくえんだま)を　三(みっ)つ　くれました。
My grandma gave me three one-hundred-yen coins.

おじいちゃんは　五百円玉(ごひゃくえんだま)を　一(ひと)つ　くれました。
My grandpa gave me one five-hundred-yen coin.

おこづかいが　千円(せんえん)に　なりました。
My allowance totaled one thousand yen.

百

hundred

[kun] none
[on] ヒャク

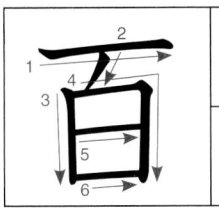

ひゃく
百
one hundred

さんびゃく
三百
three hundred

ろっぴゃく
六百
six hundred

ひゃっかじてん
百科事典
encyclopedia

千

thousand

[kun] ち
[on] セン

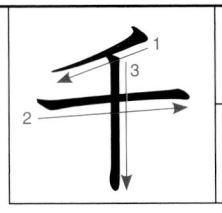

せん
千
one thousand

さんぜん
三千
three thousand

せんばづる
千羽鶴
(a string of) one thousand paper cranes

円

circle, yen

[kun] まる-い
[on] エン

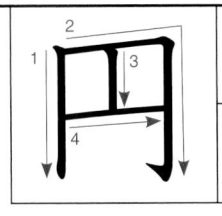

えん
円
circle, yen

ひゃくえん
百円
one hundred yen

えんしゅう
円周
circumference

玉

jewel, ball

[kun] たま
[on] ギョク

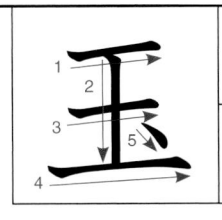

めだま
目玉
eyeball

だま
ビー玉
marble

ひゃくえんだま
百円玉
one hundred yen coin

どうぶつ Animals (耳・足・手・長)

うさぎは　耳(みみ)が　長(なが)いです。
Rabbits have long ears.

だから、小(ちい)さい　おとも　よく　きこえるのかな。
I wonder if that's why they can hear tiny sounds.

だちょうは　足(あし)が　長(なが)いです。
Ostriches have long legs.

だから、とべないけど、はやく　はしれるのかな。
I wonder if that's why they cannot fly, but can run fast.

さるは　手(て)が　長(なが)いです。
Monkeys have long arms.

だから、木(き)から　木(き)へと、どんどん　とびうつれるのかな。
I wonder if that's why they can leap from tree to tree.

でも、さるも　ときどき　木(き)から　おちるんだって。
But I heard that monkeys sometimes fall from trees, too.

手	hand **[kun]** て **[on]** シュ	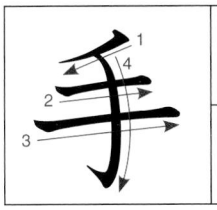

て
手
hand/arm

てがみ
手紙
letter

しゅじゅつ
手術
surgery

あくしゅ
握手する
to shake hands

足	foot, leg, pair, suffice **[kun]** あし／たーりる／たーす **[on]** ソク	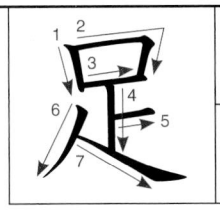

あし
足
foot/leg

えんそく
遠足
field trip

ふそく
不足
lack

た
足りる
sufficient

耳	ear **[kun]** みみ **[on]** ジ	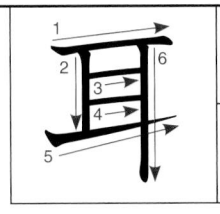

みみ
耳
ear

ちゅうじ
中耳
middle ear

じびか
耳鼻科
ear and nose doctor

長	long, eldest, chief **[kun]** ながーい **[on]** チョウ	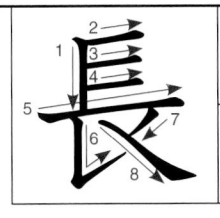

なが
長い
long

ちょうなん
長男
the eldest son

しゃちょう
社長
(company) president

せいちょう
成長
growth

力を使って Using My Strength (体・力・使)

ぼくは　まいにち　体を　きたえています。
I strengthen my body every day.

ごぜんちゅうは、
In the morning,

うでの　力を　使って、うでたてふせ。
I do pushups using the strength of my arm.

ごごは、
In the afternoon,

おなかの　力を　使って、ふっきん。
I do sit-ups using the strength of my stomach.

晩ご飯の　あとは、
After dinner,

ゆびの　力を　使って、パパと　ゆびずもう。
I do finger wrestling with my dad using the strength of my finger.

体	body **[kun]** からだ **[on]** タイ

体

からだ	たいりょく	たいいく	たいそう
体	体力	体育	体操
body	physical strength	physical education	gymnastics

力	strength, power, ability **[kun]** ちから **[on]** リョク／リキ

力

ちから	どりょく	ぼうりょく	きょうりょく	いんりょく	すいりょくはつでんしょ
力	努力	暴力	協力する	引力	水力発電所
strength, power	effort	violence	to cooperate	gravity	hydraulic power plant

使	use, servant **[kun]** つかーう **[on]** シ

使

つか	たいし	たいしかん	てんし
使う	大使	大使館	天使
to use	ambassador	embassy	angel

出る人と、入る人
People Who Exit and People Who Enter
(入・出・電)

電車や、エレベーターでは、
In trains and elevators,

出る人が先、入る人は　あと。
the people who exit should go first,
and the people who enter should go after.

入る人が　先に　入ると、出る人は　出にくいから。
If people enter first, those who are exiting cannot exit easily.

出る人が　先に　出たら、入る人も　入りやすいから。
If people exit first, those who are entering can enter easily.

入	enter, put in **[kun]** はい-る／い-れる **[on]** ニュウ	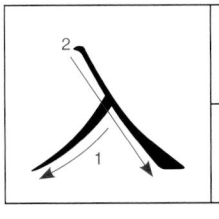

入る　入れる　入り口　入学する
to enter　to put in　entrance　to enter a school

出	emerge, put out **[kun]** で-る／だ-す **[on]** シュツ	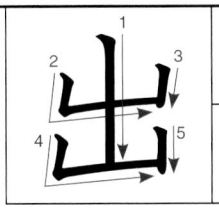

出る　出す　出口　出発
to come out　to put out　exit　departure

電	electricity **[kun]** none **[on]** デン	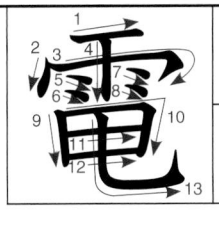

電気　電力　電車　電話　停電
electricity, electric light　electric power　electric train　telephone　blackout, power failure

休(やす)むとき When Resting (立・休・強)

しまうまは　よく　立(た)ったまま　休(やす)みます。
Zebras often rest while standing.

てきが　きたら、すぐ　にげられます。
They can quickly run away if predators come.

ライオンは　強(つよ)いので、
Lions are strong,

いつも　よこになって　休(やす)みます。
so they often rest while lying down.

でも、ゆだんたいてき!
But relaxing too much could be your worst enemy!

立	stand, establish **[kun]** た-つ／た-てる **[on]** リツ	1 2 3 4 5

立(た)つ
to stand

私立大学(しりつだいがく)
private university

組(く)み立(た)てる
to assemble

独立(どくりつ)
independence

休	rest **[kun]** やす-む **[on]** キュウ	1 2 3 4 5 6

休(やす)む
to rest, to be absent

休(やす)み
break, holiday

休日(きゅうじつ)
holiday, day off

昼休(ひるやす)み
lunch break

夏休(なつやす)み
summer vacation

強	strong, force **[kun]** つよ-い **[on]** キョウ	1 2 3 4 5 6 7 8 9 10 11

強(つよ)い
strong

強制(きょうせい)する
to enforce

勉強(べんきょう)する
to study

強調(きょうちょう)する
to emphasize

はた Flags (白・赤・青)

日本(にほん)の　はたは、赤(あか)と、白(しろ)。
The Japanese flag is red and white.

カナダ(かなだ)の　はたも、赤(あか)と、白(しろ)。
The Canadian flag is also red and white.

アメリカの　はたは、赤(あか)と、白(しろ)と、青(あお)。
The American flag is red, white, and blue.

フランスの　はたも、赤(あか)と、白(しろ)と、青(あお)。
The French flag is also red, white, and blue.

白	white, confess **[kun]** しろ／しろ-い **[on]** ハク

白(しろ)
white color

白い(しろい)
white

白鳥(はくちょう)
swan

漂白(ひょうはく)
bleach

告白(こくはく)
confession

赤	red **[kun]** あか／あか-い **[on]** セキ

赤(あか)
red color

赤い(あか)
red

赤ちゃん(あか)
baby

赤道(せきどう)
equator

青	blue **[kun]** あお／あお-い **[on]** セイ

青(あお)
blue color

青い(あお)
blue

青空(あおぞら)
blue sky

青年(せいねん)
young man/people

青信号(あおしんごう)
green (traffic) light

貝の名前 The Names of Shellfish (貝・名・前・何)

この大きい　貝の　名前は　はまぐりです。
The name of this big shellfish is *Hamaguri*.

この小さい　貝の　名前は　あさりです。
The name of this small shellfish is *Asari*.

このうずまきの　貝の　名前は　さざえです。
The name of this spiral shellfish is *Sazae*.

このきれいな　貝の　名前は　何だろう？
I wonder, what is the name of this beautiful shellfish?

貝	shellfish **[kun]** かい **[on]** (バイ)	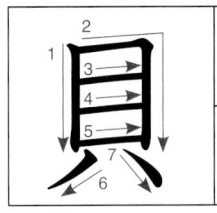

かい
貝
shellfish

かいがら
貝殻
shell

しんじゅがい
真珠貝
pearl oyster

名	name, famous, members **[kun]** な **[on]** メイ／ミョウ	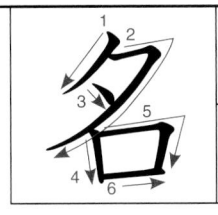

なまえ
名前
name

ゆうめい
有名な
famous

めいし
名刺
business card

前	before, front, previous **[kun]** まえ **[on]** ゼン	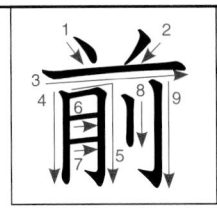

まえ
前
before, front, previous

さんねんまえ
三年前
three years ago

ぜんはん
前半
the first half

何	what **[kun]** なに／なん **[on]** none	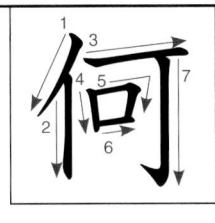

なに　か
何を買いましたか。
What did you buy?

なん
これは何ですか。
What is this?

なんにん
何人ですか。
How many people?

早(はや)おき Getting Up Early (早・朝)

早(はや)おきは　三文(さんもん)の　とく。
The early bird catches the worm.

朝(あさ)、早(はや)く　しごとを　はじめると、
If you start your job early in the morning,

しごとが　早(はや)く　おわります。
you can finish your job early.

しごとが　早(はや)く　おわれば、
If you finish your job early,

ゆっくり　あそべます。
you can spend more time having fun.

だから、朝(あさ)、早(はや)く　おきると、一日中(いちにちじゅう)　きもちいいんです。
This is why I feel great all day when I wake up early in the morning.

早	early **[kun]** はや-い **[on]** ソウ／サッ

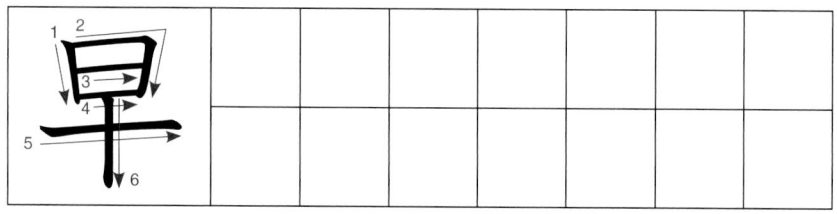

早(はや)い
early

早寝(はやね)
going to bed early

早起(はやお)きの人(ひと)
early riser

早朝(そうちょう)
early morning

早退(そうたい)する
to leave school (the office) early

朝	morning **[kun]** あさ **[on]** チョウ

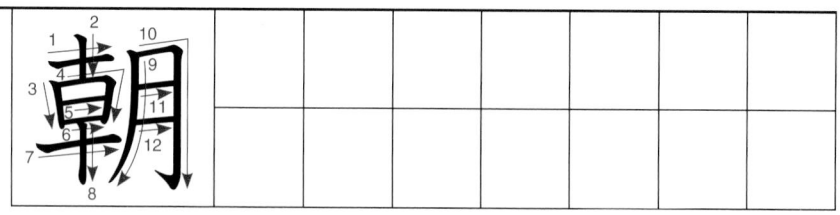

朝(あさ)
morning

朝日(あさひ)
the morning sun

朝顔(あさがお)
morning glory

朝食(ちょうしょく)
breakfast

今朝(けさ)
this morning

朝晩(あさばん)
in the mornings and evenings

夕(ゆう)がたの空(そら) The Sky at Dusk (夕・空・帰)

夕(ゆう)がたの　空(そら)は　赤(あか)いろ。
The sky at dusk is a red(dish) color.

お日(ひ)さまが、しずんで、もえているから。
That's because the sun has set and is still burning.

夕(ゆう)やけ　こやけを　うたいながら　帰(かえ)りましょう。
Let's go home while singing *Yuyake Koyake* (Evening Glow).

ああ、よかった。
Oh, I feel lucky.

帰(かえ)るうちが　あるから。
I have a home to return to.

evening

[kun] ゆう
[on] セキ

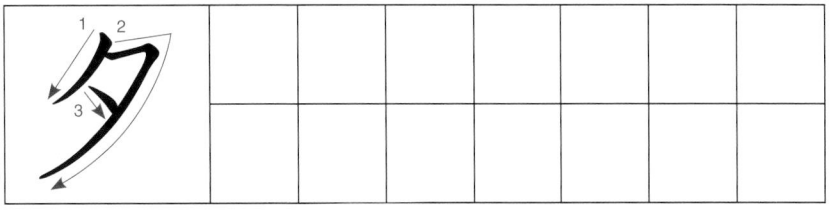

夕方(ゆうがた) evening
夕日(ゆうひ) the evening (sinking, setting) sun
夕焼け(ゆうや) evening glow
夕食(ゆうしょく) supper, dinner
七夕(たなばた) the Star Festival

sky, air, empty, vacant

[kun] そら／あ-く／あ-ける／から
[on] クウ

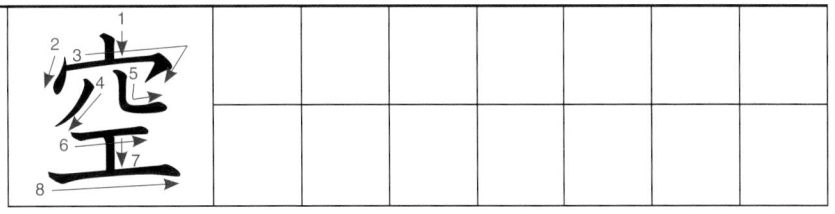

空(そら) sky
空気(くうき) air
空港(くうこう) airport
空席(くうせき) vacant seat
空手(からて) karate

return

[kun] かえ-る
[on] キ

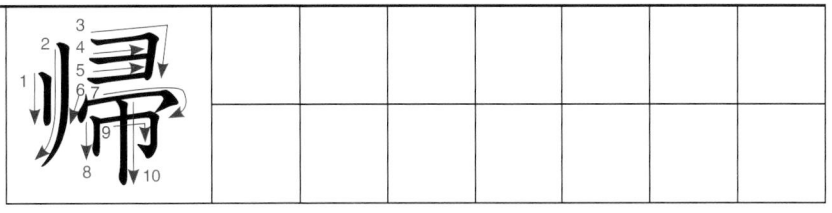

帰る(かえる) to go/come back
帰国する(きこくする) to return to one's country
帰国子女(きこくしじょ) returnee student

春ののはら Spring Field (草・花・春)

春の　のはらを　ここちよく　してくれるのは
What makes the spring field a comfortable place

草と、花です。
is the grass and flowers.

草は、うすみどりの　じゅうたん。
The grass is a light green carpet.

花は、そのじゅうたんの　きれいな　もよう。
The flowers are the beautiful patterns on that carpet.

春の　のはらで　おひるねを　すると、
If I take a nap in the spring field,

そよかぜが　のどを　くすぐって、
the breeze tickles my throat,

やさしい　お日さまが　いいゆめを　見させてくれます。
and the nice sun helps me have a pleasant dream.

草	grass **[kun]** くさ **[on]** ソウ	草

くさ
草
grass

ざっそう
雑草
weed

そうげん
草原
grassland, meadow

花	flower **[kun]** はな **[on]** カ	花

はな
花
flower

かびん
花瓶
vase

かだん
花壇
flower bed

はなび
花火
fireworks

春	spring **[kun]** はる **[on]** シュン	春

はる
春
spring

はるやすみ
春休み
spring recess

しゅんぶんのひ
春分の日
the day of the vernal equinox

竹(たけ) Bamboo (竹・馬・歩)

空(そら)を　とぶ　竹(たけ)は　何(なん)ですか？
What is bamboo that can fly in the sky?

--竹(たけ)とんぼです。
That's a take-tonbo (a flying toy made of bamboo).

のって　歩(ある)ける　竹(たけ)は　何(なん)ですか？
What is bamboo that you can get on and walk with?

--竹馬(たけうま)です。
That's a take-uma (Japanese stilts).

竹(たけ)から　生(う)まれた　女(おんな)の子(こ)は　だれですか？
Who is the girl who was born from bamboo?

--かぐやひめです。
That's Kaguya-hime (Princess Kaguya in an old Japanese story).

竹

bamboo

[kun] たけ
[on] チク

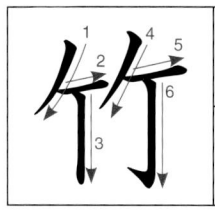

竹 (たけ)
bamboo

竹の子 (たけのこ)
bamboo shoot

竹輪 (ちくわ)
chikuwa (fish paste cooked in a bamboo-like shape)

馬

horse

[kun] うま／ま
[on] バ

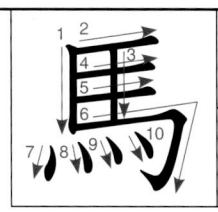

馬 (うま)
horse

馬車 (ばしゃ)
carriage

乗馬 (じょうば)
horse riding

竹馬 (たけうま)
stilt

歩

walk

[kun] ある-く／あゆ-む
[on] ホ／ボ／ブ

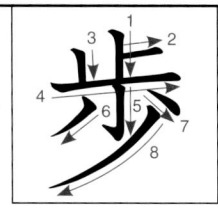

歩く (ある)
to walk

散歩する (さんぽ)
to take a walk

歩行者 (ほこうしゃ)
pedestrian

虫の音楽会 Bugs' Concert (虫・音・夜)

あきの　夜は　虫の　音楽会。
On autumn nights, there is a bugs' concert.

いろんな　音が　きこえます。
You can hear all sorts of sounds.

バイオリンみたいに
Like a violin,

キュッ　キュッ　キュッ　キュッ、キュッ　キュッ　キュッ。
Kyu kyu kyu kyu kyu kyu kyu

すずの音みたいに
Like little bells,

コロ　コロ　リン　リン、コロ　コロ　リン。
Koro koro rin rin koro koro rin.

ふえの音みたいに
Like a flute,

ピー　ピー　ヒョロロ　ピー　ヒョロロ。
Pī pī hyororo Pī hyororo

ぜんぶ　虫の　こえなんです。
They are all the voices of bugs.

虫	bug, insect **[kun]** むし **[on]** チュウ	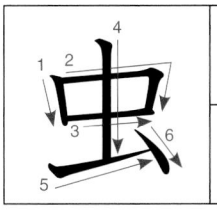						

むし
虫
bug, insect

な むし
泣き虫
crybaby

がいちゅう
害虫
harmful insects

こんちゅうさいしゅう
昆虫採集
insect collecting

音	sound **[kun]** おと／ね **[on]** オン／イン	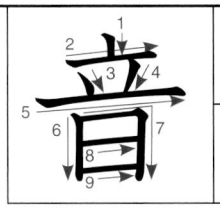						

おと
音
sound

おんがく
音楽
music

はつおん
発音
pronunciation

ぼいん
母音
vowel

ねいろ
音色
tone

夜	night **[kun]** よる／よ **[on]** ヤ	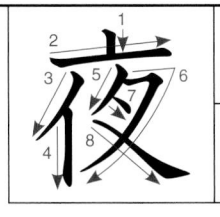						

よる
夜
night

やけい
夜景
night view

よあ
夜明け
dawn

やきん
夜勤
nightshift

村(むら)と、町(まち) Villages and Towns (村・町・家・店)

一人(ひとり)で　くらすと、さびしいです。
If I lived by myself, it would be lonely.

となりに　家(いえ)が　ないと、さびしいです。
If there was no house next to mine, it would be lonely.

家(いえ)が　いくつか　近(ちか)くに　できると、村(むら)が　できます。
If some houses were built around mine, we could make a village.

もっと　人(ひと)が　きてくれると、町(まち)が　できます。
If more people came, we could make a town.

学校(がっこう)も、びょういんも、ちかくに　できると、もう　あんしん。
If we got a school and a hospital in the neighborhood, we would feel safe.

お店(みせ)も、レストランも、できると、とても　にぎやか。
If we got stores and restaurants, it would be very lively.

ぼくの　町(まち)は、にぎやかな　町(まち)。
My town is a lively town.

村	village **[kun]** むら **[on]** そん	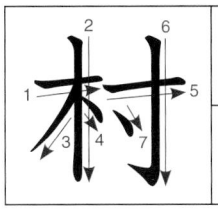

村 (むら) village　　漁村 (ぎょそん) fishing village　　村長 (そんちょう) village chief

町	town **[kun]** まち **[on]** チョウ	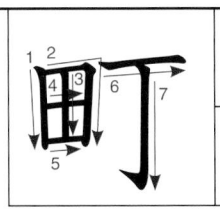

町 (まち) town　　町長 (ちょうちょう) town mayor　　町役場 (まちやくば) townhouse

家	house **[kun]** いえ／や／うち **[on]** カ／ケ	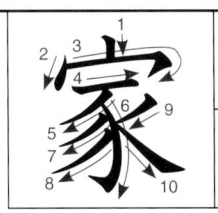

家 (いえ) house　　家族 (かぞく) family　　家具 (かぐ) furniture　　家賃 (やちん) rent

店	shop **[kun]** みせ **[on]** テン	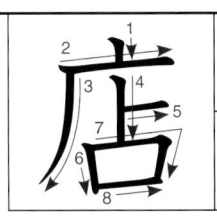

店 (みせ) shop　　店員 (てんいん) store clerk　　書店 (しょてん) bookstore

宝石 Gemstones (王・石・宝)

王さまは　宝石を　あつめるのが　大好きです。
Kings like to collect gemstones.

ダイヤモンド、ルビー、サファイアに、エメラルド。
まだまだ、たくさん　あります。
They have diamonds, rubies, sapphires, emeralds and so much more.

みんな　きれいに　光ってる。
They all shine beautifully.

キラキラ、ピカピカ、光ってる。
Kirakira, pikapika, shining.

でも、どれも　石の　なかまなんです。
But they all come from rocks.

かっこよく　きって、よく　みがくと、きれいに　なるんです。
Once you cut them nicely and polish them well, they become beautiful.

いい　名前が　あると、宝石って、よばれるんです。
If they have nice names, they can be called gemstones.

王	king **[kun]** none **[on]** オウ	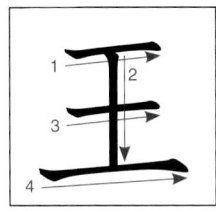

おうさま
王様
king

じょおうさま
女王様
queen

おうこく
王国
kingdom

石	stone **[kun]** いし **[on]** セキ／シャク／コク	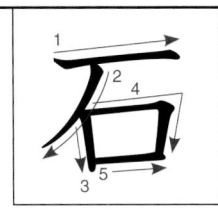

いし
石
stone

かせき
化石
fossil

じしゃく
磁石
magnet

せきゆ
石油
petroleum

宝	treasure **[kun]** たから **[on]** ホウ	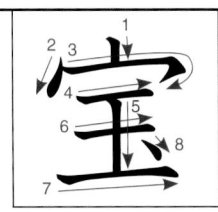

たから
宝
treasure

ほうせき
宝石
jewel, gemstone

こくほう
国宝
national treasure

糸 Threads (糸・毛・作)

毛糸は、ひつじの　毛で　作ります。
Woolen threads (yarn) are made of sheep's hair.

あったかい　セーターが　できます。
With yarn, we can make a warm sweater.

きぬの　糸は、かいこの　まゆで　作ります。
Silk threads are made of silkworms' cocoons.

きれいな　きものが　できます。
With silk, we can make a beautiful kimono.

めんの　糸は、わたで　作ります。
Cotton threads are made of cotton plants.

きもちいい　ティーシャツが　できます。
With cotton, we can make a comfortable T-shirt.

くもの　糸は、くもが　自分で　作ります。
Spider threads are made by spiders themselves.

ほかの　糸とは　ちがいます。
Their threads are different from other types of threads.

ほそくて、見えにくくて、虫が　つい　ひっかかって　しまいます。
They are thin, hard to see, and bugs get trapped in them easily.

糸	thread, string **[kun]** いと **[on]** シ

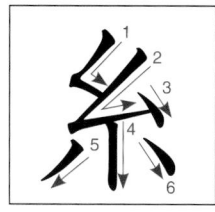

糸 (いと)	毛糸 (けいと)	糸車 (いとぐるま)
thread	woolen yarn	spinning wheel

毛	hair **[kun]** け **[on]** モウ

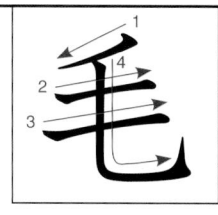

毛 (け)	髪の毛 (かみけ)	毛虫 (けむし)	毛布 (もうふ)	毛皮 (けがわ)
hair	hair (on the head)	caterpillar	blanket	fur

作	make **[kun]** つくーる **[on]** サク／サ

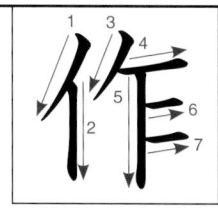

作る (つく)	作文 (さくぶん)	作家 (さっか)	作曲家 (さっきょくか)
to make	composition	writer, author	composer

てるてるぼうず Teru-Teru Bozu (雨・天・気)

あしたは　えんそく。
We have a field trip tomorrow.

雨(あめ)が　ふらないように、
To prevent it from raining,

てるてるぼうずを　作(つく)って、うたいます。
I'll make a teru-teru bozu (shiny-shiny Buddhist priest), and sing.

♪ てるてるぼうず　てるぼうず
♪ Teru-teru bozu, teru bozu

あした　天気(てんき)に　しておくれ。♪
Please make tomorrow a sunny day. ♪

雨	rain **[kun]** あめ **[on]** ウ	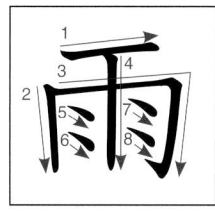	

あめ
雨
rain

おおあめ
大雨
heavy rain

こさめ
小雨
drizzle

うてん
雨天
rainy weather

天	heaven, sky **[kun]** あま- **[on]** テン	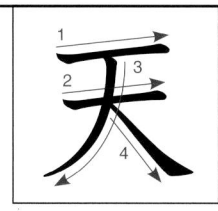	

てんごく
天国
heaven

てんじょう
天井
ceiling

てんき
天気
weather

あまがわ
天の川
Milky Way

てんさい
天才
genius

気	spirit, mind, air, mood **[kun]** none **[on]** キ	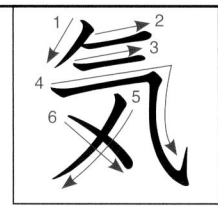	

げんき
元気な
healthy, fine

びょうき
病気
sickness

きもち
気持ち
feelings

くうき
空気
air

にんき
人気
popularity

HIRAGANA

ん n’	わ wa	ら ra	や ya	ま ma	は ha	な na	た ta	さ sa	か ka	あ a
		り ri		み mi	ひ hi	に ni	ち chi	し shi	き ki	い i
		る ru	ゆ yu	む mu	ふ fu	ぬ nu	つ tsu	す su	く ku	う u
		れ re		め me	へ he	ね ne	て te	せ se	け ke	え e
	を o	ろ ro	よ yo	も mo	ほ ho	の no	と to	そ so	こ ko	お o

KATAKANA

ン n’	ワ wa	ラ ra	ヤ ya	マ ma	ハ ha	ナ na	タ ta	サ sa	カ ka	ア a
		リ ri		ミ mi	ヒ hi	ニ ni	チ chi	シ shi	キ ki	イ i
		ル ru	ユ yu	ム mu	フ fu	ヌ nu	ツ tsu	ス su	ク ku	ウ u
		レ re		メ me	ヘ he	ネ ne	テ te	セ se	ケ ke	エ e
	ヲ o	ロ ro	ヨ yo	モ mo	ホ ho	ノ no	ト to	ソ so	コ ko	オ o